Philip Sheridan

Union General

Colonial Leaders

Lord Baltimore
English Politician and Colonist

Benjamin Banneker
American Mathematician and Astronomer

Sir William Berkeley
Governor of Virginia

William Bradford
Governor of Plymouth Colony

Jonathan Edwards
Colonial Religious Leader

Benjamin Franklin
American Statesman, Scientist, and Writer

Anne Hutchinson
Religious Leader

Cotton Mather
Author, Clergyman, and Scholar

Increase Mather
Clergyman and Scholar

James Oglethorpe
Humanitarian and Soldier

William Penn
Founder of Democracy

Sir Walter Raleigh
English Explorer and Author

Caesar Rodney
American Patriot

John Smith
English Explorer and Colonist

Miles Standish
Plymouth Colony Leader

Peter Stuyvesant
Dutch Military Leader

George Whitefield
Clergyman and Scholar

Roger Williams
Founder of Rhode Island

John Winthrop
Politician and Statesman

John Peter Zenger
Free Press Advocate

Revolutionary War Leaders

John Adams
Second U.S. President

Samuel Adams
Patriot

Ethan Allen
Revolutionary Hero

Benedict Arnold
Traitor to the Cause

John Burgoyne
British General

George Rogers Clark
American General

Lord Cornwallis
British General

Thomas Gage
British General

King George III
English Monarch

Nathanael Greene
Military Leader

Nathan Hale
Revolutionary Hero

Alexander Hamilton
First U.S. Secretary of the Treasury

John Hancock
President of the Continental Congress

Patrick Henry
American Statesman and Speaker

William Howe
British General

John Jay
First Chief Justice of the Supreme Court

Thomas Jefferson
Author of the Declaration of Independence

John Paul Jones
Father of the U.S. Navy

Thaddeus Kosciuszko
Polish General and Patriot

Lafayette
French Freedom Fighter

James Madison
Father of the Constitution

Francis Marion
The Swamp Fox

James Monroe
American Statesman

Thomas Paine
Political Writer

Molly Pitcher
Heroine

Paul Revere
American Patriot

Betsy Ross
American Patriot

Baron Von Steuben
American General

George Washington
First U.S. President

Anthony Wayne
American General

Famous Figures of the Civil War Era

John Brown
Abolitionist

Jefferson Davis
Confederate President

Frederick Douglass
Abolitionist and Author

Stephen A. Douglas
Champion of the Union

David Farragut
Union Admiral

Ulysses S. Grant
Military Leader and President

Stonewall Jackson
Confederate General

Joseph E. Johnston
Confederate General

Robert E. Lee
Confederate General

Abraham Lincoln
Civil War President

George Gordon Meade
Union General

George McClellan
Union General

William Henry Seward
Senator and Statesman

Philip Sheridan
Union General

William Sherman
Union General

Edwin Stanton
Secretary of War

Harriet Beecher Stowe
Author of Uncle Tom's Cabin

James Ewell Brown Stuart
Confederate General

Sojourner Truth
Abolitionist, Suffragist, and Preacher

Harriet Tubman
Leader of the Underground Railroad

Philip Sheridan

Union General

Dynise Balcavage

Arthur M. Schlesinger, jr.
Senior Consulting Editor

Chelsea House Publishers

Philadelphia

CHELSEA HOUSE PUBLISHERS
Editor-in-Chief Sally Cheney
Director of Production Kim Shinners
Production Manager Pamela Loos
Art Director Sara Davis
Production Editor Diann Grasse

Staff for *PHILIP SHERIDAN*
Editor Sally Cheney
Associate Art Director Takeshi Takahashi
Series Design Keith Trego
Layout by D&G Limited, LLC

B
SHE

The Chelsea House World Wide Web address is
http://www.chelseahouse.com

First Printing
1 3 5 7 9 8 6 4 2

Library of Congress Cataloging-in-Publication Data

Balcavage, Dynise.
    Philip Sheridan / Dynise Balcavage.
      p. cm. — (Famous figures of the Civil War era)
    Includes bibliographical references (p.) and index.
    ISBN 0-7910-6406-9 (alk. paper) — ISBN 0-7910-6407-7 (pbk. :
    alk. paper)
      1. Sheridan, Philip Henry, 1831-1888—Juvenile literature.
    2. Generals—United States—Biography—Juvenile literature.
    3. United States. Army—Biography—Juvenile literature. 4. United
    States—History—Civil War, 1861-1865—Campaigns—Juvenile
    literature. 5. Indians of North America—Wars—West (U.S.)—
    Juvenile literature. [1. Sheridan, Philip Henry, 1831-1888.
    2. Generals. 3. United States—History—Civil War, 1861-1865.]
    I. Title. II. Series.

    E467.1.S54 B35 2001
    973.7'3'092—dc21
    [B]   2001028880

Publisher's Note: In Colonial, Revolutionary War, and Civil War Era America, there were no standard rules for spelling, punctuation, capitalization, or grammar. Some of the quotations that appear in the Colonial Leaders, Revolutionary War Leaders, and Famous Figures of the Civil War Era series come from original documents and letters written during this time in history. Original quotations reflect writing inconsistencies of the period.

Contents

Philip Sheridan's determination and skill with horses would lead him to one day be an officer in the cavalry of the Union army during the Civil War.

The Making of a Soldier

In 1836, a group of older boys was playing in the fields near Somerset, Ohio. A five-year-old lad tagged along behind them. As they walked, the boys spotted a horse feeding in a pasture. They thought it would be fun to place their small tagalong on the frisky animal's back. As soon as the group lifted him onto the horse, the frightened animal darted off.

The horse was not fitted with a saddle or **bridle**, so there was nothing for the little rider to hold. The boy clutched the animal's mane tightly and squeezed his knees against the horse's bare back. Much to the older lads' surprise, he did not cry with fear. In fact, he seemed to enjoy riding the bucking horse. He did not fall off, either, even though he had never before ridden a horse. The animal ran for several miles, and the older boys soon lost sight of their small friend.

Once the horse got to town, he finally decided to rest. He stopped in front of a tavern that his owner often visited. People walking by in the street stopped in shock. They could not believe this tiny boy was riding alone, bareback, on such a tall, energetic horse.

A crowd gathered around the five-year-old. Little did the crowd know that this tiny horseman—Philip Sheridan—would grow up to become one of the United States' most important generals.

Philip Henry Sheridan was born in Albany, New York, on March 6, 1831. His parents, John and Mary Sheridan, moved to America from their farm in County Cavan, Ireland. They had five children: Philip, Patrick, John, Michael, and Mary. (One daughter, Rosa, died on the boat ride to the United States.) The Sheridans later moved into a three-room house on Happy Alley in Somerset, Ohio.

John Sheridan worked long, hard hours as a laborer. He helped build canals and roads, and his work kept him away from his family for long periods of time. While her husband was on the road, Mary Sheridan took care of her children and the home. She was a quiet, honest woman. She made it a point to go to church and to work hard. She made sure her children did, too.

Young Philip attended Somerset's one-room school. An Irishman named Mr. Patrick McNanly was the teacher. He had old-fashioned ideas about discipline. If just one child misbehaved, for example, he punished the entire class. He hit them one by one with a switch, a type of whip.

These punishments did not stop Philip from having a bit of fun. Sometimes, he and his friends skipped school. Instead of studying, they spent the day swimming in a nearby pond or fishing. Despite his antics, Philip was an average student. Like the other children, he studied geography, history, arithmetic, and English grammar. He loved to read, especially books about war and soldiers.

Once during a Fourth of July celebration, a veteran of the Revolutionary War named Mr. Dusenberry came to speak. Young Philip held onto his toy sword tightly. He listened carefully to every word the old war hero spoke. "I never saw Phil's brown eyes open so wide or gaze with such interest as they did on this old Revolutionary relic," said his friend Henry Greiner.

Philip decided to leave school at age 14. (This was not unusual during this time.) He took a job working at John Talbot's country store. There, he sold sugar, coffee, fabric, and other items to the customers. He earned a salary of $24 a year.

After one year, another Somerset businessman, Henry Dittoe, asked Philip to work in his dry-goods store, Fink & Dittoe. He offered Philip a huge raise—to $120 a year. Philip did not hesitate and worked at Fink & Dittoe for a few more years. He waited on customers and kept track of how much money clients owed the store. Sometimes when he looked out the shop's window, Philip could see Somerset's town **militia**, the Keokuk Rifles, practicing in the streets.

In 1846 the United States was involved in a battle with Mexico. Philip followed the Mexican-American War with great interest. He read every book, newspaper article, and story about the war and became an expert on the conflict. Customers often came into the store to talk about the war with the young clerk.

Inspired by his early horse ride and the newspaper stories about the United States' battles with Mexico, Philip dreamed of one day joining the Army. "[T]he stirring events of the times so much impressed and absorbed me that my sole wish was to become a soldier," he wrote in his memoir, "and my highest aspiration was to go to West Point. . ."

He knew, though, how hard it would be to reach this goal. Only one boy from each district

United States General Winfield Scott and his men entered
Mexico City and won the last battle of the Mexican-American
War. At the end of the war, the Treaty of Guadalupe Hidalgo
set the southern boundary of Texas and gave New Mexico and
California to the United States.

in the country was chosen to go to the United
States Military Academy at West Point, New
York.

The boy from Philip's district chosen for
West Point had failed the college's entrance
examination. Philip quickly wrote a letter to his

congressman, Thomas Richey. He asked if he could go to West Point in the other boy's place. Richey agreed but reminded Philip that he would first have to pass the difficult entrance test.

Since he had quit school several years earlier, Philip knew he would have to study very hard to prepare for the exam. Over the next few months, he spent long evenings in the back of the store, studying by candlelight. He even asked Mr. Clark, the village's schoolmaster, to tutor him. Sheridan's hard work paid off. He passed the tough test and was accepted at West Point. His dream was about to come true.

When Philip arrived at West Point, it was easy to see that most of the cadets came from wealthy families. They were well-dressed, well-behaved, and spoke intelligently.

Wearing a brown suit sewn from a sack, Philip did not make much of an impression on his well-to-do classmates. The 17-year-old was skinny and had reddish skin, and wild, wavy

Future officers of the regular U.S. Army receive their training at the United States Military Academy, at West Point, New York. Women have also studied at West Point since 1976. West Point was established in 1802 in a fortress on the Hudson River. The school was created so America would not need to rely on soldiers from other countries during wars.

Those who want to study at West Point must be nominated by their congressperson, the president, or the vice president. The U.S. government pays for cadets' tuition, room, and board. Cadets also receive a monthly stipend—a small amount of spending money. Graduates earn a bachelor of science degree.

hair. Standing just over 5' 5" tall, he was barely big enough to be admitted. All of the first-year cadets, called plebes, were given short haircuts and a uniform of brown linen to wear. Now, no matter how rich or poor the cadets were, they all looked the same.

Philip pledged allegiance to the academy on February 18, 1849. He soon learned it was easier to dream of becoming a soldier than it was to survive at West Point. The military drills were hard and tiring. The schoolwork was especially tricky. Philip had never before studied **algebra**. Now, he was being tested on this difficult subject. His friends helped him study so he could pass the exams.

To make matters worse, Philip did not feel comfortable around many of his classmates. Since many of them came from wealthy families, he felt he had nothing in common with them. Fortunately, Philip made friends with three other cadets from Ohio, named George Crook, Joshua Sill, and John Nugen.

Though he was usually quiet and polite, Philip's bad temper sometimes got him into trouble. One afternoon in 1851, during Philip's third year at the academy, the cadets were practicing their drills. Sergeant William R. Terrill of Virginia ordered Philip to line up with the rest of the men. For some reason, this command made him angry. He swung his **bayonet** at Terrill. Luckily, he stopped before he hurt the sergeant.

Sergeant Terrill told the directors of West Point what had happened. When Philip found out that Terrill had reported him, he became even angrier. He went out looking for him. Even

Philip is shown leading the way for his soldiers during a cavalry charge.

though the sergeant was much bigger, Philip started a fistfight with him. An officer broke up the scuffle.

Philip should have been dismissed from West Point for his bad behavior and violent outbursts. Instead, his superior, Captain Henry Brewertown, only punished him with a year's suspension. He was not allowed to return to West Point until the next year.

Ashamed and angry about the fight, Philip went back to work as a bookkeeper at Fink & Dittoe in Somerset. When he finally returned to West Point the next year, his attitude got worse instead of better. Still, he managed to finish his last term without getting into any major scrapes.

Philip graduated in 1853 , placing 34th in a class of 52. At last, he was a soldier in the United States Army.

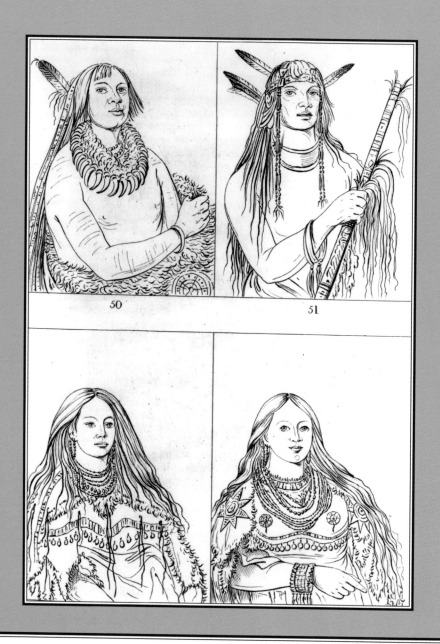

Shown here are examples of clothing, jewelry, and head-
dresses of the Comanche Indians.

First
U. S. Army
Assignments

In September 1853, Philip received his first orders from the U.S. Army. He was assigned as a brevet second lieutenant to the 1st Infantry Regiment at Fort Duncan, Texas. The fort was very close to the U.S. border with Mexico, its neighbor to the south.

Many Native American tribes had lived happily in this area for centuries. Tribes such as the Apache, Comanche, and Lipans made their homes in the present-day states of Texas, Arizona, and New Mexico in the southwestern United States. But as the country grew over the years, more people moved westward into this region and disturbed the lives of the native people. The settlers hunted so many animals that there were few left for the tribespeople. The settlers also took over a good bit of the tribes' land. The Native Americans, not surprisingly, did not welcome the white pioneers.

The Comanche people were talented horsemen. They were angry about the way the white men had invaded their land. Along with other tribes, the Comanche fought to protect their their homeland and families. Sometimes, they captured white settlers who lived in Texas and New Mexico.

The U.S. government responded to their attacks. They sent Army troops to defend its new territories and the settlers who lived there. As a result, fights between the army and tribes often broke out. Part of Philip's new duties was to protect this area from the Native Americans, even though it was originally their home.

Philip was, once again, far from home, but he was not lonely. He had several friends from West Point to spend time with.

The **barracks** were dirty and uncomfortable. When it rained, the tents often leaked. The rainwater turned the dirt floors into slippery mud. Philip disliked the barracks so much that he decided to build his own private hut. Using what materials he could find, Philip put together a small, cozy shelter. It was quite comfortable and even had a stone fireplace, chimney, and a thatched roof.

Philip's childhood horse riding experience in Somerset, Ohio, served him well in the southwest.

There was plenty of deer, wild turkeys, and antelope to be hunted in the rugged land that surrounded Fort Duncan. But fresh fruit and vegetables were hard to find. As a result, the soldiers were at risk for sauffering from scurvy. Philip and the other soldiers had to sip maguey plant juice each day so they would stay healthy and get all their vitamins. The juice smelled worse than rotten eggs, but the soldiers had to drink it anyway. One of Philips jobs was to make sure all the soldiers took their dose of juice during **roll call.**

One day in 1854, Philip and three of his men were riding along a path when a band of Apaches stopped them. The tribe members were about to attack the soldiers. When Philip saw the chief step down from his horse, he thought quickly. Wasting no time, he jumped on the bare back of the chief's horse and galloped back to Fort Duncan. As Philip fled, the Apaches shot arrows at him. He quickly returned to the scene with troops to rescue the other two soldiers. In November 1854, thanks to his hard work and bravery, Philip was promoted to second lieutenant.

In 1855, Philip was sent to the 4th Infantry in the Washington territory, in the present-day northwestern United States. There, he was in charge of a group of **mounted** infantry. During this time, many men traveled to the area to mine for gold. When the area's Yakima Indians saw these strangers armed with shovels and picks, they became frightened. They thought the white settlers were carrying weapons and wanted to go

Native Americans on horseback attacked settlers in an effort to protect their families and land.

to war with them. In order to protect their land, the Yakima often attacked these miners.

The Yakima tribe often started their raids from the Cascades, a six-mile area along the Columbia River. Philip and his men were ordered to help Colonel George Wright and his men patrol the region. They were to launch a surprise attack on the tribe.

The men sailed quietly on a ferryboat called *Belle.* The boat was equipped with a huge brass cannon that looked more powerful than it really was.

As soon as the soldiers stepped ashore and launched their attack, the Yakima fired their weapons at the men. One bullet brushed Philip's nose. It hit the soldier standing next to him. That soldier died from his wounds.

Realizing that they were outnumbered, Philip wisely told his troops to retreat. Had it not been for Philip's quick thinking and wise decision to flee, many more soldiers could have died in the attack. The next morning, Colonel Wright sent another group of soldiers to help Philip and his troops. The Yakima eventually gave up.

Sometimes Philip used brutal and unfair methods on the men he considered enemies. When he later came upon the village of a group of Cascade tribespeople, he accused the Native Americans of firing at the soldiers and killing some white settlers. The tribesmen argued that they had done nothing wrong.

Philip did not believe them. He checked each of their rifles for gunpowder. He thought gunpowder residue would prove the Native Americans had just fired their weapons. (Philip did not take into account, though, that the Cascades could have also used their guns for hunting or target practice.) In the end, he sentenced nine Native Americans to death by hanging. Soon after this the tribe stopped fighting.

After serving at Fort Yamhill and later at Fort Hoskins, Philip traveled to Yaquina Bay in 1857. The U.S. government had taken all the Native Americans' land and was forcing the tribes to move to a new home, a reservation on the Siletz River. Philip's job was to lead their move.

The Native Americans were very angry. Philip thought that letting the tribesmen keep a few guns for hunting would at least make their move a little bit easier. He promised to let them have a few rifles.

The other soldiers did not like Philip's idea. They were afraid that the tribesmen would use

Men, women, and children were taken from Africa and brought to the United States. They were then sold to plantation owners in the South. Slaves worked for little or no money in the fields and homes of their owners, and they had no rights or freedoms. Northerners opposed slavery, and the tensions between the North and South divided the country and led to war.

the weapons to attack the soldiers. Philip refused to break his promise, and the Native Americans were allowed to keep their weapons.

Philip made quite a few mistakes during his eight years as a second lieutenant. But his commanders saw that the 30-year-old was a good leader and a talented soldier. Philip had already led several successful battles. When he argued that the Native Americans should be allowed to keep their guns, he proved he was a talented **diplomat**.

In March 1861, Philip became a first lieutenant. Just a few months later, in September, Philip was promoted again, this time to captain. His superior officers sent him east to join the 13th Regiment. But there was not much time to celebrate. The Civil War had already begun.

The first battle of the Civil War took place at Fort Sumter when Confederate soldiers attacked and had their first victory in the harbor of Charleston, South Carolina.

A Divided Country

Suddenly, the United States of America was no longer united. The Civil War, or the War Between the States, started on April 12, 1861, after South Carolina soldiers fired on Fort Sumter. Even though the war had many causes, the issue of slavery was one of the most important ones. Many Southerners, or Confederates, earned their livings through their large cotton and tobacco **plantations**. They owned slaves, who picked their crops and tended their land. So, the Southerners believed in slavery. The Northerners, or Union, thought that slavery was wrong. Besides the fact that slaves were not free people, they also knew slaves were often mistreated and beaten.

After all of the excitement he had experienced in the west, Philip was a bit disappointed when he got his first Union assignment. His superiors made him the **quartermaster** of troops in St. Louis, Missouri. There, he had to oversee supplies such as tents, baggage, and food. After his thrilling western adventures, Philip thought this new work was boring. Still, he did a good job and made an excellent quartermaster.

The other army officers thought that Philip was a "modest, quiet little man." Even though he was brave on the battlefield, Philip was shy around women. He could not even work up enough courage to take a woman he liked on a carriage ride. Instead, he asked his clerk to give her the ride.

Philip's stubborn nature had not changed much since his West Point days. In March 1862, his superior officer, General Samuel R. Curtis, told Philip to buy some stolen horses. Philip thought this order was wrong. He told his commanding officer that he refused to follow through on this shady deal.

Philip was eager to find more adventurous work. He asked his commanding officers if he could be appointed as colonel of the Second Michigan Cavalry. His superiors promoted him on May 25, 1862. Philip was glad to be back on the battlefield, where he felt he belonged.

At first, the new troops under Philip's command were not impressed by their new leader. Since he was so short, they nicknamed him "Little Phil." But he soon gained their respect. Philip always spoke to his men in plain language. He told them all about his decisions and why he made them. He never sent his men anywhere that he felt would endanger their lives. Philip also felt strongly that his men should have the very best supplies.

"Men who march, scout, and fight, and suffer all the hardships that fall to the lot of soldiers in the field must have the best bodily sustenance,

This group of scouts and guides worked for the Union Army of the Potomac. They posed in their uniforms for photographer Alexander Gardner.

and every comfort that can be provided," he said.

The new colonel and his 827 men rode toward Booneville, Mississippi. The weather was hot and sticky. The soldiers wore warm, scratchy uniforms and felt very uncomfortable. The extreme heat also slowed their horses. In spite of these conditions, the Union men managed to destroy a small area of railroad to stop the Confederates from sending in more supplies and soldiers. They heated the metal rails with torches and then bent them out of shape so the Southern trains could not pass.

Just before Philip's soldiers reached Booneville at around two in the morning, a group of Confederates attacked them. Though they were greatly outnumbered, Little Phil's troops had plenty of guns and **ammunition**. They easily pushed back the enemy.

Once back safely in Booneville, the men had little time to rest. As they moved westward, they encountered still more Confederate fire. At one point, Philip wisely commanded his men to retreat because there were so many Confederate soldiers.

One of Philip's trademark skills was getting to know the area in which his men would fight.

He spent hours on horseback, exploring new ground. He sketched detailed maps of an area's railroads, bridges, rivers, roads, and hills. He wrote down and memorized every landmark. As a result, Philip knew every detail of the Booneville area.

Philip's explorations and a bit of good luck came into play as Confederate General James Chalmers's men began to attack. Just as Philip was going to order his men to move forward, a train passed by filled with grain for the soldiers' horses. The engineer blew the whistle loudly.

When Philip's soldiers saw the train, they cheered and hollered. Just a few days earlier, Philip had asked the army for more men to help his troops. Philip's soldiers had thought the train was carrying more Union troops to help them.

When the Confederates heard all of this noise, they had the same idea as Philip's men. They also thought more Union soldiers had arrived. Thinking they were outnumbered, they quickly left.

These confederate soldiers from Louisiana posed for photographer J. W. Petty at the beginning of the war.

At the same time, Philip remembered a hidden road he had discovered while scouting the Booneville region. Philip sent Captain Robert Alger and about 90 men to launch a surprise attack on the rest of the Confederates. Confronted by the charging Union soldiers, all of the remaining enemy troops retreated. Although 41

Abraham Lincoln is shown here reading the Emancipation Proclaimation to members of his Cabinet in September 1862. The final proclaimation was issued on January 1, 1863, and freed slaves in the Confederate states that were in rebellion.

of his men had died, Philip's troops had won the Battle of Booneville on July 1, 1862. They gained important ground for the Union. (Unfortunately, Captain Alger's horse hit a tree during this attack. Alger fell and broke a few ribs in the process.)

General William S. Rosecrans was impressed by Philip's good judgment. He thought Philip should be rewarded. Rosecrans and four other officers quickly sent a telegram to General Henry Halleck, the army officer who was in charge of promotions. "Brigadiers scarce; good ones scarcer. . . . The undersigned respectfully beg you that you will obtain the promotion of Sheridan. He is worth his weight in gold."

Philip's next assignment was at Rienzi, Kentucky, where he was to take charge of General Don Carlos Buell's army.

Born in a log cabin on February 12, 1809, Abraham Lincoln had little formal education, but he loved to learn and studied hard. When he grew up, he became a lawyer and a politician. The people voted him the country's 16th president in 1861. One month later, on April 12, the Civil War began.

Lincoln did not believe in slavery, which was one of the war's main causes. He wrote the Emancipation Proclamation, a document that made slavery against the law.

Just five days after the war had ended, on April 14, 1865, Lincoln and his wife went to see a performance at Ford's Theater in Washington, D.C. Southerner John Wilkes Booth shot Lincoln. The president died the next morning. Many historians think Lincoln was the country's greatest president.

Philip's friend, Colonel Archibald Campbell, congratulated him with a present—a tall Morgan horse. Jet black with three white "socks," the male horse was sturdy, quick, and graceful—just what Philip had hoped for. He named his new companion Rienzi, after the town.

When Philip reached Louisville, Kentucky, he met with Major-General William Nelson. Nelson was not feeling well, so he spoke to Philip from his bed. Nelson told Philip all about the troops he would be commanding. He was to lead the Pea Ridge **Brigade** and Hescock's **battery**. He would also soon be in charge of some new volunteer soldiers.

Then Nelson pretended to be angry at Philip. He sternly asked him why he was not wearing the correct shoulder-straps of his **rank**. Philip was confused. He said he was the colonel of the Second Michigan Cavalry and that his **shoulder straps** correctly showed he was a colonel. Then Philip got a surprise. He learned from the joking major general that he had been promoted to brigadier general. The 31-year-old went back to his room and changed his shoulder straps. His new insignia was now decorated with a star, the symbol for a general.

A Union officer (seated) is surrounded by his men at their camp.

4

Holding
the Line

While Philip got used to his new title and duties, the Southern troops were advancing into Kentucky. On the morning of September 29, 1862, Major Nelson—the man who told Philip about his promotion—was shot and killed. Much to everyone's surprise, the murderer was not a Confederate soldier. It was Jefferson C. Davis, another Union general. Nelson had argued with Davis just a few days earlier.

Davis was arrested. The Union army, including Philip, was stunned and upset. But there was too much work to do to mourn his friend. Philip was now in charge of 6,500 men—more than three times as many as he had led before. General Buell, Philip's superior, started to push his 60,000 men forward to meet the Confederates.

The Northerners were still not used to the hot Southern weather. Their scratchy wool uniforms did not help. The heat made them very thirsty. The only available water was from filthy, still pools. In order to drink the water, they had to use their handkerchiefs as filters to catch the dirt.

On October 7 near a small stream of water called Doctor's Creek, Philip received orders to conquer Peter's Hill, a high spot near the creek. Gaining this ground would give the Union forces an important advantage. Since it was a raised area, they would be able to see the enemy coming and have the advantage of aiming down at a target. Philip's men attacked.

At around two in the morning after a quick **skirmish**, the Union gained some ground, and the Confederates retreated. The Confederates were not about to give up, though. By the time the sun rose, both sides traded fire again. Gathered at the bottom of Peter's Hill, the Confederates stayed determined to defend their hill. Philip and several brigades prepared to hold their position. His men quickly dug out rifle pits to protect themselves from being shot. Sheridan ordered some of his men to go down the hill to attack. At the price of 154 lives, Union troops gained more land.

After this victory, General Rosecrans recommended that Philip be promoted to major general. Meanwhile, Rosecrans replaced General Buell. The soldiers did not like Buell very much. They were glad to be led by the man they nicknamed "Old Rosy."

Philip and his troops moved down into Tennessee. On Christmas Eve, Old Rosy told all of his generals about his new plan of attacking the Confederates. He gave them a pep talk to inspire them.

"We move tomorrow, gentlemen. . . . Press them hard! Drive them from their nests! Make them fight or run! Fight them! Fight them! Fight, I say!!"

The next day, the troops marched in the pouring rain. Many of their wagons got stuck in the mud. After this hard march, when it was finally time to go to sleep, the troops had to wear their wet uniforms to bed.

On December 30, Rosecrans decided that his men would attack near Stones River, an area south of Nashville. All of the generals, including Philip, knew they were not in the best position to fight, but they had little choice. They *had* to gain more ground for the Union. Rosecrans lined up his troops for battle. All of the generals' troops took different positions.

The Confederates opened fire on General Richard W. Johnson's men. Johnson's troops returned fire and forced the Confederates to retreat. The Union soldiers had little time to rest. Two enemy brigades were moving closer to

General William S. Rosecrans led the Union at the Battle of Stones River, south of Nashville, Tennessee.

the front. They quickly surrounded Philip's men. To make matters worse, since they had been shooting for hours, the Union soldiers were out of bullets. Luckily, another division managed to get Philip and his soldiers a few extra cartridges.

Even though the men seemed doomed, General Rosecrans commanded them to hold the line. Philip was certain that he and his troops would be killed. He decided not to die without putting up a fight. The Confederates attacked the men three times. Since they were standing on a flat bed of limestone, the shots rang out very loudly. The bullets bounced off the rocks and killed many Union soldiers. Even during this intense battle, Philip stayed calm and gave his men orders. He told them where and when to fire and where to move.

Philip knew his troops had to retreat somehow, but there seemed to be no escape. He was faced with a hard decision; he knew that some men would have to face the enemy's fire in order to save the rest. He asked Colonel George Roberts and his brigade to cover the rest of the soldiers' retreat.

Roberts bravely obeyed Philip's orders and led his men into position. He was immediately shot and killed. His sacrifice saved the lives of most of the Union soldiers. In just four hours, more than 1,600 of Philip's soldiers were killed–almost half of his men. Rosecrans's men then quickly gathered up about 50 cannons, which they used to keep back the enemy.

Now on safer ground, Philip's troops had a few minutes to load their weapons. But the Confederates did not let up–they fired constantly.

By 5:00 P.M., the shooting finally stopped. Exhausted and worn down, Sheridan and his men–those that were left–had achieved Rosecrans's goal. They had held the Union line.

The next morning, December 31, 1862, was so cold that some of the wounded men were frozen to the ground. Most of the men had not slept or eaten. They were shaken by the previous day's gruesome battle. They felt lucky to be alive. A supply train came and brought more ammunition to the troops.

Later in the day the Confederates attacked once again. This time, they were no match for the Union. With their new supply of bullets, the Union Soldiers shot 1,700 Confederate soldiers in just an hour. The Battle of Stones River was finally over. The rest of the Confederates retreated, and the Union had won once again.

Even though he had lost many men, the Battle of Stones River was a major victory for the Union and for Philip. It gave the soldiers an important position. General Ulysses S. Grant, the commander of the entire army, knew that the victory would not have happened without Philip's wise decisions and leadership. Philip had helped Rosecrans hold the line. He had sacrificed some of his men so that many more would be saved. He had made difficult decisions and had bravely faced death right alongside his men.

"It showed what a great general can do even in a subordinate [lower] command; for I believe Sheridan in that battle saved Rosecrans' army."

Over the next several months, things remained quiet, at least compared to the Battle of Stones River. From November 23 to 25, 1863, Philip pushed his men to the base of Missionary Ridge. Philip's superiors told him not to lead his men to the top of the ridge. Soldiers on higher ground–the Confederates, in this case–always have an advantage over the men below. But as usual, Philip only followed rules when he felt they made sense. This time, he had a better idea. Disobeying his orders, Philip told his men to move to the top of the ridge. This was a very dangerous decision.

His men chased after the enemy. One enemy soldier shot a horse (not Rienzi) right out from under Philip, but even this did not stop him. Even though he had disobeyed his commanders and had risked his mens' lives, Philip's men drove the Confederates from Missionary Ridge.

Philip disobeyed his commanders and pushed his men to
Missionary Ridge near Chattanooga, Tennessee. He drove
the Confederates from the area and claimed victory.

They staked their flags at the ridge's top and proclaimed victory. After this win, General Grant put Philip in charge of all the Union cavalry units–about 10,000 men.

There was no time to celebrate. The Union forces needed to take hold of Chattanooga, Tennessee. Two of the South's railroads, the East Tennessee and Virginia, ran through this town. The trains kept their troops throughout the country well-stocked with food, supplies, and men. Taking Chattanooga would cut off their supplies. It would not be easy. A high circle of mountains and a roaring river surrounded the town. And General Bragg had plenty of Confederate troops to protect Chattanooga.

In May 1864, Philip's men captured the South's trains. They damaged about 10 miles of tracks so the cars could not move any further. They also cut the **telegraph** wires so the Confederates could not send any messages. In the process, they freed 400 Union prisoners. Not long after, Philip's forces wrecked the Richmond,

Philip won an important battle against General Jeb Stuart at Yellow Tavern, near the Confederate capital of Richmond.

Fredericksburg, and Potomac railroads and captured about 50,00 Southern prisoners. Thanks to all this destruction, the Union took Chattanooga and cleared a safe path for Grant's forces to advance to Petersburg.

Further along at Yellow Tavern, Philip's forces fought with the enemy army. His men killed the Confederate leader, Jeb Stuart, who was also a graduate of West Point. His loss was a crushing blow for the Confederates. Stuart was regarded in the South as one of the Confederates' finest soldiers and leaders.

Grant was impressed by all that Little Phil had accomplished in just three weeks. In August 1864, Grant gave Philip a new, important assignment. He was to lead the Army of the Shenandoah in Virginia.

Like Chattanooga, the Shenandoah Valley was another major source

In 1619 about 20 African men were captured and brought to America to work as slaves. As the United States grew, many large farms, called plantations, were formed in the South. These huge cotton, tobacco, and sugar farms needed many workers. The owners used slaves to pick their crops and care for their estates. Slaves were sometimes beaten, overworked, and separated from their families.

In 1724, the Quakers, a religious group, said they thought slavery was wrong. Many people, especially Northerners, followed their example and spoke out against this cruel practice. Slavery eventually divided the country and was a major cause of the Civil War.

of supplies to the Confederate army. The South had held it now for three years. The valley was also important, because it was a clear way for the Union to get to Washington, D.C. Philip's job was to chase the enemy to the south and to destroy all of their supplies.

Sheridan's army attacked the Confederate forces on September 19 near Winchester. They took over the valley in a matter of just a few days. To celebrate his latest victory, he gave his horse, Rienzi, a new name. From this point on, he called his trusty Morgan "Winchester."

Under Grant's orders, Philip's men destroyed all the barns, factories, stores, and equipment in the valley. The people who lived there now were almost starving. Some people, including some Northerners, thought Philip's destruction was wrong. But Philip thought the Southerners had brought about these bad conditions themselves.

President Abraham Lincoln was so impressed by Philip's new successes, that he wrote him a letter to congratulate him. "Have just heard of your great victory," he wrote. "God bless you all, officers and men. Strongly inclined to come up and see you."

Philip led the charge through the Shenandoah Valley to make sure that the Union held on to their hard-won land.

More Northern Victories

In just a few days, the Shenandoah Valley had been lost by the Confederates. But they were not about to give up their ground without a fight. About a month after the Shenandoah Valley was captured, the Confederates heard that Fighting Phil, as he was now nicknamed, was at a meeting in Washington. Without the advantage of Philip's savvy leadership, the Southern troops knew it was the perfect time to launch an attack. They surprised the Union forces at Cedar Creek.

But the Confederates got more than they expected. By that time, Philip had already returned from Washington and was staying at Winchester. When he heard the gunshots ringing out, he quickly hopped on his horse and rode to the field to give his men a fighting pep talk. "Face the other way boys!" he yelled. "We are going back!"

Inspired by their leader's words and energy, the Union troops launched a counterattack. They caught the enemy soldiers off-guard. Even though they held onto their hard-won Shenandoah Valley, the price was great. More than 17,000 Union solders were killed or wounded.

Members of Congress wanted to thank Philip for his brave and intelligent leadership. They asked him to come to Washington again, so they could hold a victory parade. A poet named Thomas Buchanan Reed even wrote a poem in Philip's honor.

Philip smoked a cigar as he watched the procession from a balcony. Once in a while he raised his hat to the crowds and soldiers. Many horsemen paraded by their honored leader. They held flags that stood for each of Philip's

Union Civil War hero Ulysses S. Grant became the 18th president, serving from 1869 to 1877.

many victories. As they trotted by Philip, they raised their swords in a salute of respect.

In early spring 1865, Philip and Grant took part in a final battle against the forces at Richmond, Virginia. Tired, hungry, and worn down from all the fighting, the Confederates were no match for the polished Union forces. The Union had cut off all escape routes, so the Confederates had no choice but to retreat.

Confederate General Robert E. Lee surrendered the Army of Northern Virginia to Union general Ulysses S. Grant at Appomattox Court House, Virginia, ending the Civil War.

Confederate General Robert E. Lee and his exhausted men left Richmond on April 3, 1865. Philip and his men followed them. The Confederates were ready to attack, but decided not to when they saw line after line of eager Union soldiers. "My God!" Lee exclaimed about his own forces. "Is the army dissolved?"

But the war was not over yet. The Confederates later found enough strength to attack Philip's men at Five Forks. But once again, they were no match for the Union soldiers. The Northern forces won yet another battle. They also took the Confederates' cannons and about 3,000 prisoners. It wasn't long before Five Forks also belonged to the Union. The Confederates marched in the dark to Appomattox, Virginia, where they knew that Lee, their worn down leader, was staying.

On April 9, General Grant and Philip met at the town of Appomattox Court House, Virginia. When

The Union army wanted to capture the Shenandoah Valley because most of the Confederates' supplies came from the region. Today, looking at the peaceful, green Shenandoah Valley, it is difficult to imagine the Civil War's bloody battles. Many people from all over the world visit its famous tree-covered Blue Ridge mountains and drive through Shenandoah National Park. From the Park's Skyline Drive, visitors can see the valley in which Philip Sheridan and his men once fought.

Grant asked Philip where General Lee was, he pointed to a house nearby. Union soldiers surrounded it. Grant went inside, while Philip and his men waited anxiously on the front lawn. A few minutes later, Grant called the soldiers inside. There, they watched General Lee surrender. The bloodshed was finally over. The North had won the Civil War.

In 1870, Philip explored the wilderness surrounding Yellow-stone River in Montana.

After the Glory

Even though the war was over and the North had won, some Confederate forces were still active in Texas. Confederate General E. Kirby Smith commanded these rebellious men. General Grant knew the best man to handle the situation was Philip, so he ordered him to go to Texas.

A celebration parade was planned in Washington on May 23 to honor the army's of Ulysses S. Grant, Philip Sheridan, and William Tecumseh Sherman. Philip wanted to stay and march with the other generals and enjoy some peace and quiet after all the fighting. But Grant's command was firm. Philip had to go to Texas—and fast. Surprisingly, once he got there, Kirby surrendered without a struggle.

Since he had traveled so far, Philip decided to make good use of his time in the Lone Star State. The French army was gathered across the Rio Grande River in Mexico. Their leader, Emperor Napoleon III, wanted to make his friend, Hapsburg Archduke Ferdinand Maximilian, Mexico's emperor. To prove to the French that he would invade Mexico if necessary, Philip marched his soldiers along the Rio Grande. He wanted to show the French how large and strong his army was. Philip's plan worked. The French army left after they saw Philip's forces.

In 1869, Philip's friend, Ulysses S. Grant, was elected president. Not long after, Grant made Philip a lieutenant general. As part of his new duties, Philip took a ship across the Atlantic Ocean to study the German armies who were at war with France. President Grant wrote a letter to introduce Philip to his German hosts. He called his friend and comrade "one of the most skilled, brave, and deserving soldiers developed by the great struggle through which the United States Government had just passed."

Philip's trip to Europe was quite an adventure. After visiting the cities of London, England; Brussels, Belgium; and Berlin, Germany, Philip met the German king, William I. The 73-year-old ruler liked Philip so much that he gave him a personal tour of his headquarters. King William wanted to know what Americans thought of Germany's war with France, called the Franco-Prussian War.

While Philip was observing the fighting along with the king, he gave his hosts some military advice. On August 18, 1870, while looking through a spy glass, he could see some French soldiers sneaking up on the Germans. They were about to fire. Philip told the German general Otto Von Bismarck, who spoke English, about the upcoming attack.

"Sheridan had seen it from the beginning," the general recalled. "I wish I had so quick an eye."

After leaving Germany, Philip also traveled to Constantinople (now Istanbul, Turkey) and Greece. Once back in his home country, he was sent to Chicago to lead the military headquarters. He brought back a wonderful souvenir to remember his trip—an English greyhound. Unfortunately, the dog did not enjoy a long life. He was killed in a hunting accident not long after he came to his new American home.

In 1870, Philip visited an unusual area near the Yellowstone River in Montana. There, he saw amazing forces of nature. Even though he had traveled around the world and had seen many unique things, the area's **geysers,** hot springs, and hot lava thrilled Philip. Excited by the beauty, he found some people to explore this wilderness. In 1872 it became the United States' first national park.

Philip returned to his post in Chicago. Just a few days later, on October 8, 1871, a fire started in a barn in a run-down neighborhood. The Great Chicago Fire destroyed Philip's headquarters and personal items, along with a good bit of the rest of the city. The city was suffering from a **drought** and most of the city's buildings were made from wood, which caused the fire to spread quickly. By the time the fire burned out the next day, it had destroyed a three-and-a-half-mile area and caused $200 million worth of damage.

Philip was ordered to take charge of the city to stop people from looting businesses after the fire. His troops patrolled Chicago's streets and stopped thieves from robbing the few stores that had not burned. He and his men also handed out food, blankets, and other supplies to thousands of people who had lost their homes in the blaze. Philip also tried to influence local merchants to keep their prices fair and not cheat the people who lost everything in the fire.

In 1873 a political riot was taking place in New Orleans, Louisiana. Philip was sent in to keep the peace. About 38 people were killed, including 34 African Americans. Philip wanted

Crowds of people rushed across the Randolph Street Bridge during the Great Chicago Fire. Philip was in charge of the military headquarters in Chicago at the time, and his troops assisted residents following the disaster.

to set the record straight. On August 2, Philip sent General Grant a telegram about the riot. "The more information I obtain, the more revolting it becomes, it was no riot. It was an absolute massacre by police . . ."

Since Philip was so busy, he found little time for romance. But when he met dark-haired Irene Rucker in spring 1874, his thoughts turned to love. The two got along well, even though Philip was 22 years older than Irene. On June 3, 1875, the couple got married and they settled in Washington, D.C.

After spending so many years living with gruff soldiers, married life was a welcome change. Irene had a positive affect on Philip. His bad temper and loud voice seemed to disappear overnight.

As the years passed, Philip became more sickly. Part of the problem was his weight. He loved to eat and often ate too much. He weighed more than 200 pounds, yet he was just over 5' 5". Sometimes, it was hard for the once-lively soldier

Irene Rucker grew up in Washington, D.C. Her grandfather, father, and two brothers had served in the army. She was a devout Catholic, who had attended parochial schools in Washington, D.C., and Philadelphia, Pennsylvania.

Irene married Philip on June 3, 1875, in a simple ceremony. They had four children: Mary, twins Irene and Louise, and Philip Henry Jr. When her husband died in 1888, she decided never to marry again. "I would rather be the widow of Phil Sheridan than the wife of any man living," she said. She died in 1938.

to breathe. In March 1888 he had his first heart attack at age 57.

On June 1, 1888, Congress awarded Philip the army's highest military rank. He became a full general and could now wear four stars on his uniform. Around this time, he started to write a book about his many adventures and travels.

Philip's family thought moving from the hot, uncomfortable weather in Washington, D.C., would help make the general healthier. They made a trip to Nosquitt, Massachusetts, so Philip could rest by the sea.

The weather was cooler there, and the ocean breezes made Philip feel more comfortable. He relaxed in the little cottage and even got a chance to review the pages of his autobiography. "I hope that some of my old boys will find the book worth the purchase," he said after he had reread his manuscript.

The next evening, on August 5, 1888 at 9:30, Philip suffered a serious heart attack. An hour later, he was dead.

Philip's body was taken in a funeral procession to Arlington National Cemetery. His new horse, Guy, trotted near his master's casket with the general's boots placed backward in the stirrups. Philip Henry Sheridan was buried after a 17-gun salute. It was fitting that after devoting so much of his life to the army, his final place of rest would be among fallen soldiers.

GLOSSARY

algebra–an advanced area of mathematics.

ammunition–bullets and cannon balls used in guns and cannons.

barracks–housing in which military troops live.

battery–a set of guns or cannons.

bayonet–a long sword.

bridle–a sort of "leash" used to guide a horse.

brigade–a small group of soldiers.

diplomat–a person who helps two sides agree on an issue or get along better.

drought–a period of little or no rainfall, when an area's water supply dries up.

geyser–a hot spring that shoots water up into the air.

militia–an army made up of ordinary citizens.

mounted–riding on horseback.

plantation–a large farm where crops such as cotton, peanuts, and tobacco are grown.

quartermaster–an officer who is in charge of a troop's clothing, food, and other supplies.

rank–a soldier's position in the army.

roll call–when an officer takes attendance of soldiers.

scurvy–a disease that people get when they do not consume enough vitamin C.

skirmish–a quick, fairly informal battle.

shoulder straps–accessories that soldiers wear on their shoulders to show their rank.

telegraph–A system of communication that existed before the telephone. Operators sent messages through a series of wires.

CHRONOLOGY

1831	Philip Henry Sheridan is born on March 6 in Albany, New York.
1853	Graduates from West Point; in September, he is assigned as a brevet second lieutenant to the 1st Infantry Regiment at Fort Duncan, Texas.
1861	Promoted to captain.
1862	Promoted to colonel of the Second Michigan Cavalry; promoted to brigadier general; and then to major general. Leads the Battle of Stones River.
1863	Leads the Battle of Missionary Ridge.
1864	Leads cavalry Army of the Potomac; leads the Battle of the Wilderness; leads the Army of the Shenandoah.
1865	Forces Confederates to retreat at Petersburg; stops Lee at Appomattox Court House; Confederacy surrenders on April 9.
1869	Promoted to lieutenant general by President Grant.
1870	Travels to Europe to study German armies.
1875	Marries Irene Rucker on June 3.
1883	Named commander in chief of the army.
1888	Promoted to full general–the highest military rank. After suffering a heart attack, he dies on August 5 in Nosquitt, Massachusetts.

CIVIL WAR TIME LINE

1860 Abraham Lincoln is elected president of the United States on November 6. During the next few months, Southern states begin to break away from the Union.

1861 On April 12, the Confederates attack Fort Sumter, South Carolina, and the Civil War begins. Union forces are defeated in Virginia at the First Battle of Bull Run (First Manassas) on July 21 and withdraw to Washington, D.C.

1862 Robert E. Lee is placed in command of the main Confederate army in Virginia in June. Lee defeats the Army of the Potomac at the Second Battle of Bull Run (Second Manassas) in Virginia on August 29–30. On September 17, Union general George B. McClellan turns back Lee's first invasion of the North at Antietam Creek near Sharpsburg, Maryland. It is the bloodiest day of the war.

1863 On January 1, President Lincoln issues the Emancipation Proclamation, freeing slaves in Southern states. Between May 1–6, Lee wins an important victory at Chancellorsville, but key Southern commander Thomas J. "Stonewall" Jackson dies from wounds. In June, Union forces hold the city of Vicksburg, Mississippi, under siege. The people of Vicksburg surrender on July 4. Lee's second invasion of the North during July 1–3 is decisively turned back at Gettysburg, Pennsylvania.

1864   General Grant is made supreme Union commander on March 9. Following a series of costly battles, on June 19 Grant successfully encircles Lee's troops in Petersburg, Virginia. A siege of the town lasts nearly a year.

Union general William Sherman captures Atlanta on September 2 and begins the "March to the Sea," a campaign of destruction across Georgia and South Carolina. On November 8, Abraham Lincoln wins reelection as president.

1865   On April 2, Petersburg, Virginia, falls to the Union. Lee attempts to reach Confederate forces in North Carolina but is gradually surrounded by Union troops. Lee surrenders to Grant on April 9 at Appomattox, Virginia, ending the war. Abraham Lincoln is assassinated by John Wilkes Booth on April 14.

FURTHER READING

Clayton, Nancy. *Strange But True Civil War Stories*. Los Angeles: Lowell House, 1999.

Harmon, Dan. *Civil War Generals*. Philadelphia: Chelsea House, 1998.

Herbert, Janis. *The Civil War for Kids*. Chicago: Chicago Review, 1999.

Moore, Kay. *If You Lived at the Time of the Civil War*. New York: Scholastic, 1994.

Tracey, Patrick Austin. *Military Leaders of the Civil War*. New York: Facts on File, 1993.

PICTURE CREDITS

INDEX

Note: **Boldface** numbers indicate illustrations.

ABOUT THE AUTHOR

A freelance writer, **DYNISE BALCAVAGE** is also the author of six other books: *Ludwig van Beethoven, Steroids, The Great Chicago Fire, The Federal Bureau of Investigation, Janis Joplin,* and *Saudi Arabia.* Three other books, *Gabrielle Reece, Iowa,* and *Iraq,* are scheduled for publication later this year. She also updated a book called *Culture Shock!: Syria* after traveling extensively in that country. Additionally, Balcavage has written many magazine articles, essays, poems, short stories, and book reviews. She occasionally does poetry readings and teaches writing classes in the Philadelphia area.

Balcavage has visited Jordan, Israel, Morocco, and Turkey, and has spent a great deal of time in Europe, especially in France. She earned a B.F.A. in visual arts from Kutztown University and an M.A. in English from Arcadia University. She lives in Philadelphia.